Bebikaan-Ezhiwebiziwinan Nimkii
The Adventures of Nimkii

Stacie Sheldon

Illustrated by Rachel Butzin
Translated by Margaret Noodin

HIDDEN TIMBER BOOKS

Stacie Sheldon/Hidden Timber Books
6650 West State Street, #D98
Milwaukee, WI/53213
www.hiddentimberbooks.com

Book design by Jade Burel using BookDesignTemplates.com (© 2017)

Illustrations by Rachel Butzin | Translations by Margaret Noodin

Ordering Information: Special discounts are available on quantity purchases by corporations, associations, and others. For details, contact the publisher at the address above.

Bebikaan-Ezhiwebiziwinan Nimkii: The Adventures of Nimkii / Stacie Sheldon — Second Edition

ISBN 978-1-7365519-2-9

Printed in the United States of America

Onji-ozhibii'igaade
Dedication

Nindoodamawaa ningashe, Cindy Sheldon. Mashkawizi, zaagi'iwed miinawaa
gikendang ezhi-ganawendang apiitendaagwak.

I dedicate this book to my mother, Cindy Sheldon. She is strong, loving,
and knows how to fight for what matters.

For a word and pronunciation guide visit:
http://www.ojibwe.net/nimkii-book/

To hear and learn Twinkle Twinkle Little Star in Ojibwe revitalization of indigenous languages visit:
http://ojibwe.net/songs/childrens-songs/twinkle-twinkle-little-star/

Akawe gikendaagwad
Introduction

Ojibwemowin (or Anishinaabemowin as it is called by many speakers) is the first language of a vast landscape that includes most of Michigan and Ontario, northern Minnesota and Wisconsin and even parts of Alberta. Sadly, the language is endangered with speakers being lost more quickly than are being gained. The language is beautiful and ancient and conveys a unique way of seeing the world.

This book is an extension of greater work to not only help preserve the language but to use it. A living language is one that is being used and we invite anyone who is interested to learn and use these wonderful sounds and support the revitalization of indigenous language.

A Note about Dialects: This version uses what is commonly known as a western double vowel spelling system, but we honor and recognize all the dialects of Anishinaabemowin and hope this story will be shared widely.

Mii wa'aw Nimkii.
This is Nimkii.

Izhinikaazhaa Nimkii.
She is named Thunder.

Apii noondang animkiikaag miidash minawaanigozid.
When she hears thunder, she feels happy.

Mino-bakaani-ezhiwebiziwinan maadakamigak apii bimibizoyang odaabaaning.
Fun adventures start when we ride in the car.

Mii wa'aw misko-odaabaan.
This is a red car.

Aaniin enaazod odaabaan minwenimad?
What is the color of the car you like?

Gidandawendaan ina bimibizoyan odaabaaning?
Do you want to ride in the car?

**Nimkii gaye
Nala wiijikiwenyindiwag.**
Nimkii and Nala are friends
with each other.

**Aangodinong Nimkii gaye
Nala aadawa'amidiwag
Naadawe-Ziibing.**
Sometimes Nimkii and Nala travel
by boat on the Huron River.

Ayaanaawaan oshki "jiimaan."
They have a new "canoe."

**Onji-minawaanigoziwag jiimaan
initaagwak dibishkoo "jiimshin."**
They are happy because canoe
sounds like "give me a kiss."

Ningikendaamin wayiiba waa-iskigamizigeyang apii onaabanak.
We know we will be boiling sap soon when there is a hard crust on the snow.

Ziigwang, Nimkii onandawaabamaan aninatigoon.
In spring, Nimkii looks for maple trees.

Gigikendaan ina aninaatig-aniibiish izhinaagwad?
Do you know how a maple leaf looks?

Nimkii omiigwechiwi'aan aninaatigoon.
Nimkii thanks the maple trees.

Miidash ozhiga'aan miinawaa iskigamizigeyang.
Then we tap the trees and gather sap to boil it down into sugar.

Nindozhitoonmin zhiiwaagamizigan gaye ziinzibaakwad.
Then we make syrup and sugar.

Zhiiwaagamizigan minwaagamin! Ziinzibaakwad minopogwad!
The maple syrup is delicious! The sugar is delicious!

Akina gegoon ozhaawashkwaawan miinawaa onizhishing ziigwang.
Everything is so green and pretty in the spring.

Nimkii odaa-biijimaandaanan akina gegoon.
Nimkii has to smell everything.

Memindage mamaangibiisaa.
Even when there are big drops of rain.

**Nimkii ogwaashkwanodawaan
mitigibanan aangodinong.**
Nimkii jumps onto trees sometimes.

**Ishpigwaashkwani. Aaniin epiitaag
ishpigwaashkwaniyan.**
She can jump high.
How high can you jump?

**Simba ina owii-gwaashkwanodawaan
mitigibanan?**
Will Simba jump onto the tree?

Niibinong Nimkii ominwendaan ji-babaamibatood.
In the summer Nimkii likes to run.

Ominwendaan babaamibatwaazhaad Finnan miinawaa Niyayan.
She likes to run with Finn and Niya.

Awenen maamwi-gizhiibatood?
Who is running the fastest?

Gigashkigizhiibatoo ina? Gizhiibatoon dash!
Can you run fast? Run fast!

Aangodinong zhaashaawanibiisiwag o'odaminotawaawaan Nimkiiyan.
Sometimes the swallows play with Nimkii.

Aangodinong zhaashaawanibiisiwan o'odaminotawaan Nimkii.
Sometimes Nimkii plays with the swallows.

O'odaminotaadiwag.
They play with each other.

Babaazhaashaawanibiisewag.
They go about gliding over the water.

Onzaam gizhiibizowag wenji-bwaadebibinindwaa!
They are so fast is the reason they are unable to be caught!

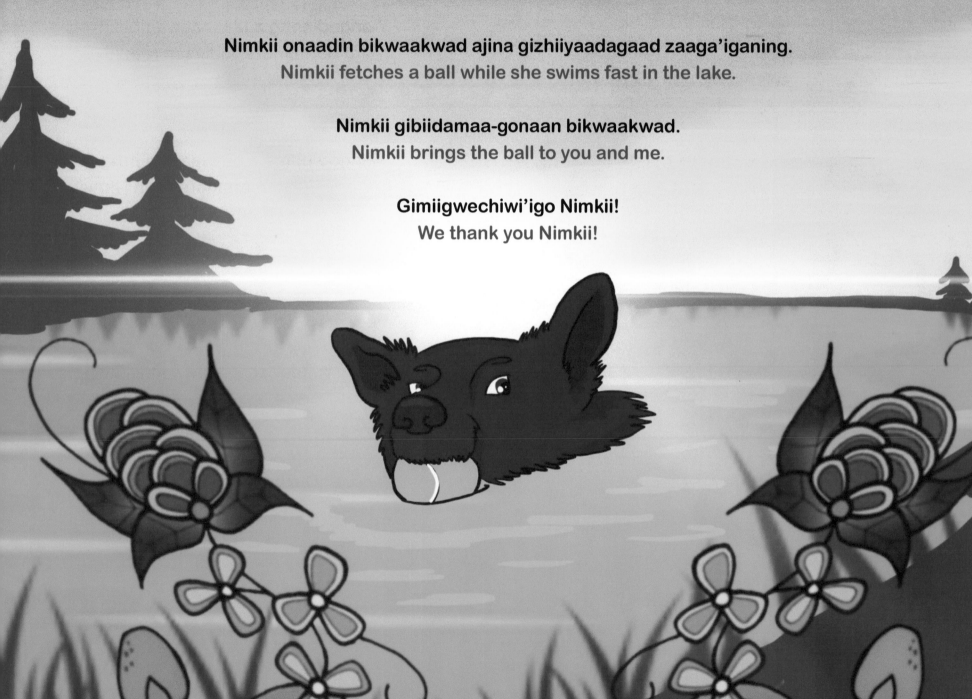

Awenen waa-nakwebidood i'iw bikwaakwad?
Who will catch that ball?

Nimkii onaadin bikwaakwad ajina gizhiiyaadagaad zaaga'iganing.
Nimkii fetches a ball while she swims fast in the lake.

Nimkii gibiidamaa-gonaan bikwaakwad.
Nimkii brings the ball to you and me.

Gimiigwechiwi'igo Nimkii!
We thank you Nimkii!

**Apii gizhaateg Nimkii minwendang
ji-babaamosed oodenaang,**
On a hot day Nimkii likes to
walk around town.

Miidash ji-dakishing miijid dekaag.
Then to cool off she
eats ice cream.

**Aaniin dinowa dekaag
minwendaman?**
What kind of ice cream
do you like?

Nimkii ogii-mikaan miskominikaan.
Nimkii found a raspberry patch.

Nimkii omikawaan miskominan gaye memengwaan.
Nimkii found raspberries and butterflies.

Aaniin minik miskominag waabamadwaa?
How many raspberries do you see?

Aaniin minik memengwaag waabamadwaa?
How many butterflies do you see?

Awenen waawaata'am-oonangwaa?
Who are they waving at us?

Awenen waawaazakonesewaad niibinong dibikak?
Who are they flashing in the summer night?

Aawiwag waawaatesiwag igo!
They are fireflies!

Dagwaagin mino-izhiwebag ji-nandokawechiged agwajiing.
Autumn is a good time to look for tracks outside.

Aaniin minik wiijiiwaaganag nandawaabam-angwaa megwayaakong?
How many friends can we find in the woods?

Giwaabamaag ina baapaase, agongos, gaag, waabooz miinawaa waawaashkeshiwag?
Do you see the woodpecker, chipmunk, porcupine, rabbit and deer?

Awenen ishpabid mitigong?
Who is sitting high up in the tree?

Ajidamoo!
Squirrel!

**Nimkii ina baapi'igod iniw
ajidamoon?**
Is Nimkii being laughed at by
that squirrel?

**Waatebagaa
Waatebagaa-giizisong.**
The leaves are bright
in September.

**Binaakwe`igeyang
Binaakwe-giizisong.**
We rake in October.

Nimkii odamino dagwagig.
Nimkii plays in fall.

Ditibise aniibiishing.
She rolls in the leaves.

Aniin daa-ateg anaami-aniibiishing?
What could be under the leaves?

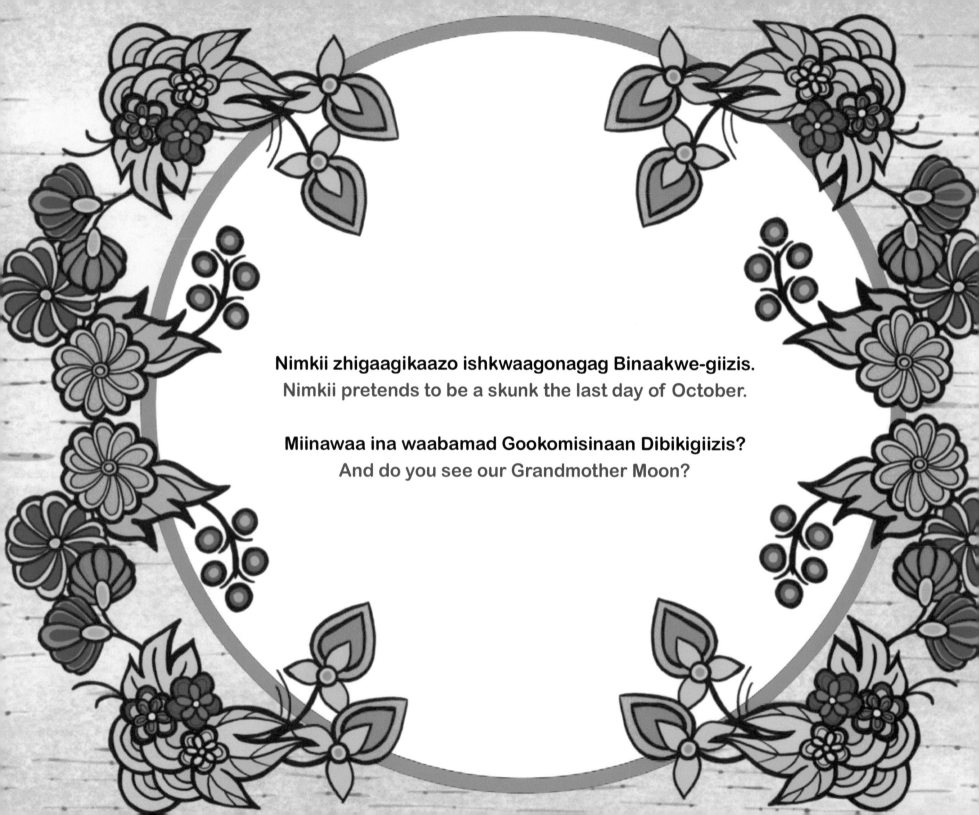

Nimkii zhigaagikaazo ishkwaagonagag Binaakwe-giizis.
Nimkii pretends to be a skunk the last day of October.

Miinawaa ina waabamad Gookomisinaan Dibikigiizis?
And do you see our Grandmother Moon?

Biboong, Nimkii ominwendaan zoogipog
In winter, Nimkii likes when
it is snowing

miinawaa Anishinaabeg aadizookewaad biinjaya'iing.
and the Anishinaabe people are
telling stories inside.

Omaaminonenimaan goonensan minopogozinid.
She realizes snowflakes
taste good.

Nimkii aabajitoon odaabaa'igan ji-zhooshkwajiwed.
Nimkii uses a toboggan to slide.

Gidaabajitoomin Anishinaabe-ikidowin "odaabaa'igan" apii Zhaaganaashiimoyang.
We use the Anishinaabe word "odaabaa'igan" when we speak English.

Nimkii ominwendaan ganawaabamaad anangoon biboong.
Nimkii likes to look at the stars in winter.

Owaabamaan Wenabozho-anangoon gaye Ma'iingan-anangoon.
She sees the Wenabozho constellation and the Wolf constellation.

Nimkii nagamo "Epaaskaakonesed epaaskaakonesed agaashiin anangens."
She sings "Twinkle Twinkle Little Star."

Gidandawendaan ina nagamoyan?
Do you want to sing?

Nimkii miinawaa Nala niikomowag ajina odaminowaad.
Nimkii and Nala growl when they play.

Ozhiibiigibidoonaawaa zhiishiib-odaminowaagan gooning.
They pull on the toy duck in the snow.

Agongos oganawaabamaan.
A chipmunk is watching them.

25

**Baanimaa bebikaan-ezhiwebiziwin
Nimkii zhiibaangwashi.**
After a big adventure Nimkii
takes a quick nap.

**Nimkii zhiibaangwashi
besho ishkodeng.**
Nimkii takes a quick nap by the fire.

Aaniindi waa-zhiibaangwashiyan?
Where would you like to
take a quick nap?

Minogwaaman.
Good night.

Gizaagi'in.
I love you.

Gimiigwechiwi'ininim
Acknowledgements from Stacie Sheldon - Author

I would like to say miigwech or thank you to everyone who has been part of my language journey.
Special thanks to Margaret Noodin who has been my collaborative partner for nearly 15 years on the creation and evolution of ojibwe.net. My friend through thick and thin and the most magical writer of words I have ever known. This book would not exist without her.

I want to acknowledge the Miskwaasining Nagamojig (Swamp Singers). A special group of ladies that gets together to sing songs in Ojibwe and support one another. We stand strong together and always remember what joy our language can bring. Marsha Traxler Reeves, Margaret Noodin, Linda Purchase, Jasmine Culp, Jasmine Pawlicki, Karen Schaumann, Nancy Morehead, Michelle Saboo, Andrea Wilkerson and all who have come before us in song and all who will come after us.

My deep love and gratitude also to my many relatives including my Aunt Dawn who has always loved me like her own, and the powerful and loving community of friends that I have come to know in my lifetime.

Stacie Sheldon - Author

Chitwaadewegekwe nindizhinikaaz Anishinaabemong. Ajijaak nindoodem. Cheboygan, Michigan nindoonjibaa. Ann Arbor, Michigan nindaa.

Honor Beat Woman is my name in Anishinaabemowin. I am crane clan. I am originally from Cheboygan, Michigan. I currently reside in Ann Arbor, Michigan.

Stacie has a career as a User Experience Researcher and Designer. She is a co-founder and leads the technical development of www.ojibwe.net.

She also served on the Board of Directors for American Indian Services in Lincoln Park, Michigan for the last 14 years. Stacie is a member of Miskwaasining Nagamojig (the Swamp Singers), a women's hand drum group whose lyrics are all in Anishinaabemowin (Ojibwe).

Nimkii - Thunder - The Adventurous Dog

Nimkii was born in the spring of 2010 and is half German Shepherd and maybe half Black Labrador. She was adopted by Stacie as a puppy and she is 100% awesome. Except for when she rolls in the mud or other stinky things. Nimkii loves her grandparents and family and all of her doggie friends including Roscoe, Ella, Niya, Finn, Cooper, Mazie, Tizzi, Seger, Morgan, and Nelson. This past year her friends Chester and Nala walked on, we treasure their memories.

Margaret Noodin – Translator

Margaret Noodin received a PhD in Literature and Linguistics, an MFA in Creative Writing and bachelor's degrees in English and Education at the University of Minnesota. She is currently Professor of English and American Indian Studies at the University of Wisconsin-Milwaukee where she also serves as the Associate Dean of the Humanities and the Director of the Electa Quinney Institute for American Indian Education.

She is the author of Bawaajimo: A Dialect of Dreams in Anishinaabe Language and Literature, and two bi-lingual books of poetry in Anishinaabemowin and English: Weweni and What the Chickadee Knows. Her poems have been anthologized in New Poets of Native Nations, Sing: Poetry from the Indigenous Americas, Poetry Magazine, The Michigan Quarterly Review and Yellow Medicine Review. To see and hear current projects visit www.ojibwe.net where she and other students and speakers of Ojibwe have created a space for language to be shared by academics and the native community. Margaret was born in Colorado and grew up in Chaska, Minnesota and has been blessed with many mentors and teachers as she has worked in language and education. She has spent a lifetime learning and teaching the language of her ancestors. Her family names include: O'Donnell, Orr, Hill, Bernard, Bean, Lavallee and Monplasir. She identifies as American, Anishinaabe, Irish and Metis.

Rachel Butzin - Illustrator

Rachel Mae Butzin is an Indigenous artist whose work is a reflection of her diverse heritage as well as her love of the environment, comic books, and pop culture. Rachel is a graduate of Michigan State University and currently resides in South Dakota with her family, where she is an art teacher at a Native American School.

Rachel has been illustrating children's books, working with different clothing companies, has collaborated with several musicians on animations for music videos, as well as logo designs for several companies.

Anishinaabemowin
Word List

For audio and word list, go to **www.ojibwe.net/nimkii-book**

1. Agongos(ag) – Chipmunk(s)
2. Ajidaamoo(g) – Squirrel(s)
3. Anang(oog) – Star(s)
4. Animosh(ag) – Dog(s)
5. Baapaase(g) – Woodpecker(s)
6. Bikwaakwad(oon) – Ball(s)
7. Bimibizo – To go for a ride
8. Dekaag – Ice Cream
9. Ditibise – To roll around
10. Gaag(wag) – Porcupine(s)
11. Gijigijigaaneshiinh(yag) – Chickadee(s)
12. Gookomisinaan Dibikigiizis – Our Grandmother Moon
13. Goonens(an) – Snowflake(s)
14. Jiimaan(an) – Canoe(s)

15. Mamaangibiisaa – To rain in big drops
16. Mememgwaa(g) – Butterfly(ies)
17. Mikan – To find something
18. Mikaw – To find someone
19. Minawaanigozid – To be happy
20. Miskomin(ag) – Raspberry(ies)
21. Nakwebidoon – To catch something
22. Nashke! – Look!
23. Nimkii – Thunder
24. Odaabaan(ag) – Car(s)
25. Waabooz(oog) – Rabbit(s)
26. Waawaashkeshi(wag) – Deer
27. Waawaata'amaw – To wave at someone
28. Waawaatesi(wag) – Firefly(ies)
29. Zhaashaawanibiisi(wag) – Swallow(s) (bird)
30. Zhiibaangwashi – To nap
31. Zhooshkwajiwe – To slide
32. Zoogipon – It is snowing

HIDDEN TIMBER BOOKS

For more publications visit:
http://www.hiddentimberbooks.com/

Publishing stories rooted in Place that offer readers social and historical context, cultural and philosophical insights.

#YourStoryMatters

CPSIA information can be obtained
at www.ICGtesting.com
Printed in the USA
BVHW050747100222
628526BV00001B/3